Aesop's Fables

Collect all the Everystories:

Aesop's Fables

Retold by
Malorie Blackman

Illustrated by
Patrice Aggs

SCHOLASTIC
Home of the Story

For Neil and Elizabeth, with love

Scholastic Children's Books,
Commonwealth House, 1–19 New Oxford Street,
London WC1A 1NU, UK
a division of Scholastic Ltd
London ~ New York ~ Toronto ~ Sydney ~ Auckland
Mexico City ~ New Delhi ~ Hong Kong

First published by Scholastic Ltd, 1998

Text copyright © Oneta Malorie Blackman, 1998
Illustrations copyright © Patrice Aggs, 1998

ISBN 0 590 54382 2

Published and bound by
Cox & Wyman Ltd, Reading, Berkshire

8 10 9

The right or Malorie Blackman and Patrice Aggs to be identified as
the author and illustrator respectively of this work has been asserted
by them in accordance with the Copyright, Designs and
Patents Act, 1988

Contents

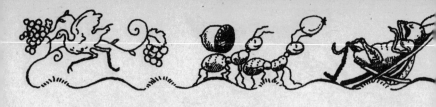

FOXY AND THE
SOUR GRAPES

Foxy was walking along the dusty road one day, minding his own business and thinking foxy thoughts, when he came across a high vine. Now this vine was laden down with big, beckoning grapes.

"My! You look juicy. You look sweet! You look good enough to eat,"

said Foxy, licking his lips.

So up he hopped, he jumped, he leapt. But he just couldn't reach those grapes. He took a running jump at them. He bounced. He vaulted. He sprang. But nothing doing.

Slinking away, Foxy had a growl, a scowl, a glower. He said, "I bet those grapes are yuck and sour!"

Some people comfort themselves by pretending that they don't want what they can't have or can't get.

THE SUN AND THE
NORTH WIND

"When you get right down to it, I'm stronger than you," said the North Wind.

"You really think so?" smiled the Sun.

"All right then, I'll prove it," said the North Wind. "You see that man down there with a coat on? I bet I can

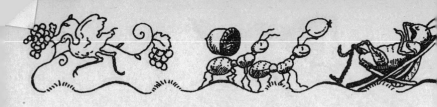

blow his coat right off. Watch this!"

And the North Wind blew and Blew and BLEW. He blew around the man's head, around his legs, around his back and his chest, trying to tear his coat off. But the man just pulled his coat even more firmly around him, shivering against the cold.

"D'you mind if I have a try?" said the Sun.

And he shone. Warm, soft, golden rays.

"What funny peculiar weather!" said the man, unbuttoning his coat.

And the sun shone some more.

Bright, light rays everywhere.

"I'm melting," the man gasped. And he pulled off his coat and slung it over his shoulder.

"I win! I win!" grinned the Sun. "Deal with that!"

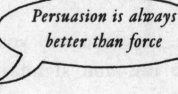

Persuasion is always better than force

THE TORTOISE
AND THE HARE

"Tortoise, you are so slow! How can you stand it?" asked the Hare.

"I like my pace. I have time to admire the sky and the flowers and listen to the breeze blow."

"Phooey!" Hare snorted. "When I run I get to where I'm going almost

before I leave!"

"Oh, for goodness' sake," Tortoise said. "Speed isn't everything. I bet if we had a race right here and now, I'd have a good chance of beating you. How about a race over the hill and back?"

Hare roared with laughter. "You and me have a race? You wouldn't stand a chance."

"We'll see." Tortoise smiled.

But Hare didn't reply. He'd already started running. It wasn't long before Hare was way, way out in front.

"Why am I hurrying? That tortoise

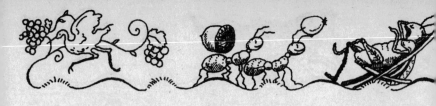

is so slow, I could run this race fifteen times before he's even finished once. I might as well take it easy." So Hare settled down for a nap. "I can have a little sleep and still beat that tortoise – easy peasy, lemon squeezy!" And he closed his eyes and started snoring.

A little while later, the tortoise plodded past the sleeping hare and continued on his way, over the hill and back again. Hare awoke and raced to catch up but he'd left it too late. Tortoise crossed the finish line first and beat him.

Slowly but surely often wins the race. Focus and concentration will often bring success where natural talent but no determination will not.

THE LION
AND THE FOX

An old lion came up with a plan to get himself some food without having to run and sweat and work for it. He lay in a cave and moaned and groaned for all he was worth.

"Ooh, my head hurts. Ooh, my back aches. Ooh, my paws are so sore. I'm ill! I'm sick! I'm dying!"

It wasn't long before animal after animal came to see how the poor lion was doing. But the moment they entered the lion's cave, he pounced on them and gobbled them up.

One day a fox came to call. He stood outside the cave and asked, "How are you, Lion? Feeling better?"

"Not at all," croaked the lion. "Come in and see for yourself."

"I would," said the wise fox, "if it wasn't for the fact that I can see plenty of tracks going into your cave and not a single one coming out again!"

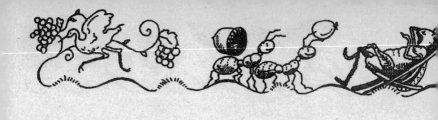

Look before you leap.

THE LION
AND THE MAN

A lion and a man were travelling along a road together. They started arguing about which one of them was the stronger, the more powerful. They came across a statue at the side of the road – a statue of a man strangling a lion with his bare hands.

"You see that!" said the man. "That

just proves my point. Over there is a statue of a man overpowering a lion."

The lion smiled a wry, dry smile. "If lions bothered to carve and sculpt, I'm sure you'd see a lot of statues of lions with humans under their paws."

Each person who describes an event can't help but put his or her own slant on it. We all believe our own point of view is more true than anyone else's.

THE ANTS
AND THE
GRASSHOPPER

It was summer. And while the ants gathered seeds and nuts for the cold days to come, grasshopper jumped about and sang happily in the sun. But summer didn't last forever. Winter came. It blew cold and hard and fierce. Poor grasshopper was starving. There was no food anywhere. Dying of

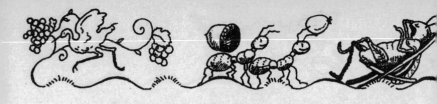

hunger and cold, he made his way to the ants and begged them for something to eat.

"And what were you doing in summer while we were working hard to gather up all this food?" the ants asked.

"I was singing," the grasshopper replied.

"Really!" said the ants, less than impressed. "Well, as you sang then, you can dance now — and see where that gets you."

A smart person puts something away for when times are bad.

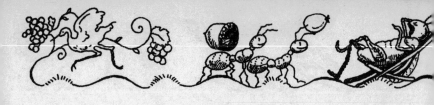

THE WOLF'S
DINNER

A wolf waited until the goatherd went away to have his dinner and then he pounced. He caught up a kid in his powerful jaws and turned to run away and devour his catch in private.

"Wait a moment," said the kid. "I know you're going to eat me, but I have also heard that you play the flute

more sweetly than any other animal alive. I'm sure if you were to play now, many more of my family would willingly follow you."

So the wolf picked up the goatherd's flute and started to blow. The noise alerted the goatherd who came back with help and drove the wolf away.

"Serve me right," said the wolf as he ran off. "I'm a butcher. I had no business being a musician as well."

If you stick to what you do well, success will surely follow.

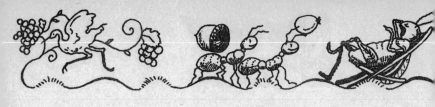

THE VIXEN
AND THE LIONESS

"Really! Is that all you could manage?!" scoffed the vixen. "Look at my lovely cubs. I have loads! Five beautiful cubs. You only have a measly one."

"Only one," came the reply. "But a lion."

Quality, not quantity, is what counts.

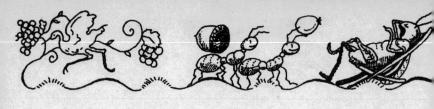

The Dog
and the Bone

A dog stole a juicy bone and ran off with it in his mouth. He came to a calm river where, looking down, he was surprised to see another dog staring back at him. This other dog also had a bone in his mouth, but the other dog's bone looked much more meaty and juicy.

"Give me that bone. It's mine!" the first dog growled. And he lunged for it.

As his own bone fell into the river and was swept away, too late the dog realized that he had been growling at his own reflection.

Being too greedy can often lose you what you already have.

At Dinner with Stork and Fox

Fox invited the stork over for dinner. He served delicious soup in a wide, flat soup bowl. Try as she might, Stork couldn't pick up a drop in her long beak, much less swallow anything.

"Not eating, Stork?" asked Fox, enjoying himself. "Here! Let me help."

And Fox licked up Stork's portion as well. Poor Stork had to go home hungry but she was determined to get her own back. The following week, Stork invited Fox to dinner.

"I'm cooking loads, so come hungry," said Stork.

Ravenous, Fox sat down to dinner. He could smell wonderful smells coming from Stork's kitchen.

"I've cooked one of your favourites," said Stork.

And in she came with two long, thin pitchers of stew.

"Eat up!" said Stork, dipping her

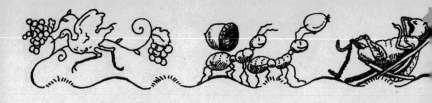

beak into the pitcher and eating her fill.

But try as he might, the fox couldn't get a bite. He couldn't get his snout into the thin pitcher.

"Not hungry? Here! Let me help you," said Stork. And she ate Fox's portion as well, as he slunk back home with his tail between his legs.

If you are spiteful to others, you shouldn't be surprised when they are spiteful to you.

THE LION, THE FOX AND THE DONKEY

One day a lion, a fox and a donkey went hunting. After a hard day's work, they had caught and killed a number of animals.

"Now then," said the lion to the donkey. "If you will divide up the food, we can each take our share and go home."

The donkey divided the food into three equal portions. But when the lion saw this, in a rage he turned on the donkey and killed him. The lion turned to the fox.

"If you will divide this food into two portions, we can each take our share and go home."

The fox put the best, tenderest, choicest meats into one pile for the lion, taking only a few morsels for himself.

"Who taught you to divide up food like that?" asked the lion.

"Oh, I don't know. What happened

to the donkey might have had something to do with it!" came the fox's
reply.

*It is wise to learn from the
mistakes of others.*

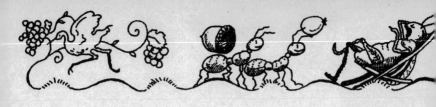

THE GOOSE WHO
LAID GOLDEN EGGS

A man once owned a goose who laid one gold egg each morning. But as time passed, the man grew more and more impatient with waiting for his special egg each day.

He said to himself, "I bet that goose has got a huge lump of gold inside."

So he killed the goose and opened it

up and surprise, surprise! There was
no gold, just normal, ordinary goose
innards.

*If it's not broken,
don't fix it! If something is working
well, leave it alone.*

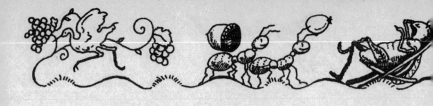

THE FOX
AND THE CORN

A farmer caught the fox who had been stealing corn from his corn field and decided to have some fun. He tied some kindling to the fox's tail and set it alight. How he laughed as the poor fox ran around in agony. But his laughter soon turned to anguish and tears as the fox, distraught with pain, ran

up and down the farmer's corn field setting all his corn alight and destroying his crop for that year.

We should never give way to spite.

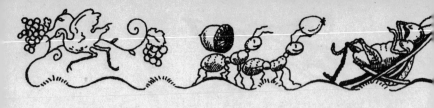

THE SHIPWRECK

There was a terrible storm. A ship was being pummelled by the savage wind and huge waves and soon it began to sink. Everyone on board jumped off the ship and started swimming for their lives. All, that is, except one man. He stayed on board as the ship was going down, crying out,

"Save me. Athena, save me and I will place gems and the finest foods and wines on your altar."

From the sea below, another man called out to him, "Don't leave it all to Athena. Let your arms and legs do some of the work as well!"

Don't leave your future solely to destiny or others. You have to put some effort in for yourself too.

41

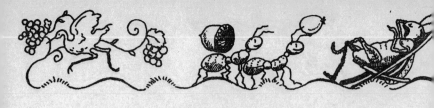

THE MOUSE
AND THE LION

A sleeping lion was wakened up by a mouse running over him. Catching the mouse with one paw, the lion was just about to snack on her when the mouse begged, "Please don't eat me. I'm not even a morsel for a big lion like you. If you spare my life, I promise that some day, in some way, I

will repay you."

The lion thought about it and, admiring the mouse's courage, said, "You're right. You aren't even a mouthful. You're barely worth me opening my mouth! So I'll let you go. But I don't see what a tiny thing like you could ever do to repay me, so you'll forgive me if I don't hold my breath!"

The lion let the mouse go nevertheless.

A few days later, the lion was caught in a huntsman's net and couldn't get out, no matter how hard he struggled. The mouse saw that the

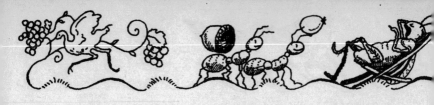

lion was trapped. Without a word, she chewed through first one section of rope, then another and another. Very soon, the lion was free.

"Thank you, friend mouse. I thought I was done for," said the lion.

"I told you I'd be able to repay you one day," said the mouse. "Aren't you glad now that you spared my life?"

Don't mock those smaller and more helpless than you. One day you may need their help. Kindness brings rewards.

THE FOX AND THE WILD BOAR

A fox was out for a walk one day when he came across a wild boar, sharpening his tusks against the trunk of a tree.

"Why on earth are you doing that?" asked the fox. "There's nothing to fear here. There's no danger anywhere around us, no huntsmen in sight."

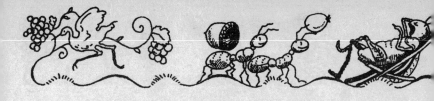

"Which is why I'm doing it now," said the boar. "When there is danger around me, I won't have time to stop and sharpen my tusks."

Be prepared.

THE FROGS
WANT A KING

"We want a king!"
"We should have a ruler!"
"We need a king!"
The frogs went to Zeus and asked him to give them a king. Fed up with their complaining, Zeus threw an old stick into their pond home.
"He's not much of a king."

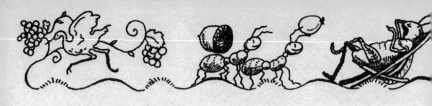

"He just lies around all day."

"He never speaks and never moves."

"What use is he?"

So the frogs went back to Zeus and complained about the king they'd been given. Furious at their attitude, Zeus threw a water snake into the frogs' pond and the water snake set about eating as many frogs as he could get his fangs into.

Be careful if you complain about someone in charge. You might end up with someone much worse to take their place.

THE BIRD
AND THE BAT

A bird sat in her cage by a window. She waited silently for the sun to set and the sky to get dark before she started singing. A bat flying past the window asked the bird, "Why do you never sing until it gets dark?"

The bird replied, "When I was free, I sang in the daytime and that's how I

got caught. So it taught me a lesson and now I only sing at night."

"Well, it's a bit late to take precautions now," said the bat. "You should've been more careful before you were caught."

It's no good taking care after the damage has already been don Be watchful before, not afterwards.

Mother Crab and her Daughter

"Must you walk like that?" a crab mother complained to her daughter. "Don't walk sideways. It's so undignified, so common! Walk properly."

"I certainly will, mother," said the daughter crab. "Just as soon as you show me how it should be done."

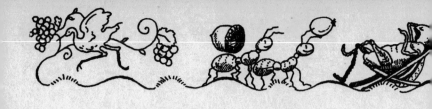

*Example is
the best teacher.*

SNAKE IS FED UP!

"Zeus! Zeus! I hate to complain, but I'm fed up!" said the snake.

"Fed up with what?" Zeus sighed.

"All day long people walk all over me," the snake wailed. "They trample on my tail, they march on my middle, they hop on my head. That's why I'm fed up."

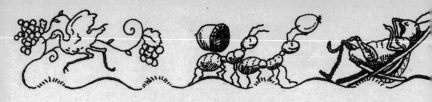

Zeus replied, "If you had bitten the first man who trod on you, the next one would've thought twice about doing the same thing."

Sometimes the best tactic is to show that you mean business from the start.

THE STAG'S MISTAKE

As a stag stood drinking from a spring, he noticed his reflection in the water.

"Look at my gorgeous antlers!" he said to himself, turning his head this way and that. "They are big and broad and quite stunning. But look at my spindly legs. They're so knobbly and

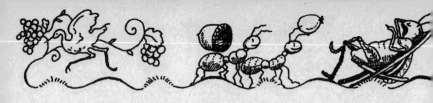

skinny, I can hardly bear the sight of them."

Suddenly, from out of nowhere a lion appeared. The stag turned and ran for his life. On the open plain, he put a great deal of distance between himself and the lion. But when he reached wooded country, his antlers became caught up in the branches of a tree so that he couldn't run any further. In fact he couldn't move at all. As the lion was about to pounce, the stag thought bitterly, "My legs which I scorned almost saved my life. And my antlers which I was so proud of have

been the death of me."

> *In bad times, we find out who is a true friend and who is the real enemy.*

THE LARK
AND HER FAMILY

A lark made her nest in a field of corn so that her young would have plenty to eat until they were fully fledged and ready to fly. One day, the farmer came to the corn field and, seeing that his crop was ripe and dry, he said to himself, "I'd better get my friends together to harvest my corn."

One of the lark chicks heard him and told his mother.

"We don't have to go just yet," said the lark.

The next day, the farmer came to inspect his corn and he said to himself, "I shall get all my relatives to help me harvest my corn."

The lark chick told his mother what the farmer had said.

"We still have a little time," said the lark.

The next day the farmer came to inspect his corn again, by which time the corn was so ripe the ears of corn were

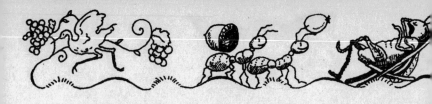

dropping off in the heat of the sun.

"Right! That does it!" said the farmer. "I'm going to hire some men and gather up the crop myself first thing tomorrow."

When the lark chick told his mother what the farmer had said, the lark said, "Now it is time to go. When a man relies on himself rather than on his family and friends, then things definitely get done."

If you want to make sure something gets done, do it yourself.

THE RIVERS
AND THE SEA

All the rivers got together and complained to the sea, "When we reach you, our waters are fresh and clean and drinkable. And then you turn us silty and salty."

"If it upsets you," said the sea, "don't come!"

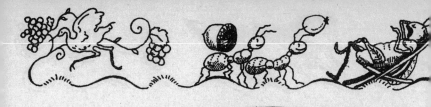

What cannot be cured, must be endured. What we can't change, we just have to put up with.

THE THIRSTY
CROW

A crow was so thirsty she thought she would surely die from it if she didn't find water soon. She came across a large pitcher that had a small amount of water at the bottom. Try as she might, the crow's beak couldn't reach the bottom of the pitcher and the pitcher was far too heavy for her

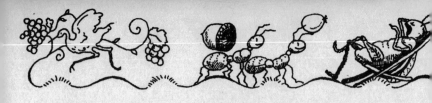

to tip over. So the crow stood back and had a think. Then she had an idea. She picked up a pebble with her beak and dropped it into the pitcher. Then another and another. She kept at it until the water was at the top of the pitcher instead of the bottom and then she could drink.

Thinking first before rushing in will get the job done.